THE 12 BIGGEST BREAKTHROUGHS IN
COMPUTER TECHNOLOGY

by Marne Ventura

12
STORY
LIBRARY

www.12StoryLibrary.com

12-Story Library is an imprint of Peterson Publishing Company and Press Room Editions.

Produced for 12-Story Library by Red Line Editorial

Photographs ©: GSGrigoriev Ruslan/Shutterstock Images, cover, 1; anuchit sookseanthaworn/Shutterstock Images, 5; Bettmann/Corbis, 6; Georgios Kollidas/Shutterstock Images, 7; hujiie/Shutterstock Images, 8; Morphart Creation/Shutterstock Images, 9; Library of Congress, 10, 11; Frederick News-Post/AP Images, 12; CYLU/Shutterstock Images, 13; AP Images, 15; vseb/Shutterstock Images, 17; Benson HE/Shutterstock Images, 19, 29; atm2003/Shutterstock Images, 20; Denis Rozhnovsky/Shutterstock Images, 21; LeoSad/Shutterstock Images, 22; Ken Wolter/Shutterstock Images, 23; Konstantin Chagin/Shutterstock Images, 24; Eric Risberg/AP Images, 25; Twin Design/Shutterstock Images, 26; Nucleartist/Shutterstock Images, 27, 28

ISBN
978-1-63235-012-1 (hardcover)
978-1-63235-072-5 (paperback)
978-1-62143-053-7 (hosted ebook)

Library of Congress Control Number: 2014937356

Printed in the United States of America
Mankato, MN
June, 2014

Go beyond the book. Get free, up-to-date content on this topic at 12StoryLibrary.com.

TABLE OF CONTENTS

1

ABACUS BECOMES FIRST MACHINE USED FOR COUNTING

We might think of computers as sleek electronic devices with lots of programs and games. But a computer is any machine that uses numbers to process information. By this definition, people have been using computers for thousands of years.

The first computers came about because people needed a better way to count. Before then, people counted using their fingers or pebbles. As much as 30,000 years ago, people made tally marks on bones or sticks. But these methods only worked for small numbers. People started to develop tools for counting larger numbers.

In approximately 190 CE, the Chinese invented the first machine used for counting. The Chinese abacus had a wooden frame with beads that moved along metal rods. The beads in each row have a specific value, such as ones, tens, and hundreds. The beads can be moved to add, subtract, multiply, and divide. This simple device set the stage for more complicated tools to come.

SALAMIS TABLET

Before the abacus, merchants used counting boards to calculate large sums. One of the earliest known counting boards was the Salamis Tablet. Babylonian traders started using it in approximately 300 BCE. They drew lines on a slab of marble. Columns of lines showed place value. Merchants used the tablet to count, add, and subtract larger numbers.

13

Number of vertical wires on a Chinese abacus. Each wire has seven beads.

- Introduced in approximately 190 CE in China.
- Used to add, subtract, multiply, and divide.
- Led to more complex machines to process data.

The abacus is still used in parts of the world for quick math calculations.

2

PASCAL INVENTS FIRST AUTOMATIC CALCULATOR

A teenager invented the first automatic calculator. In 1642, 19-year-old Blaise Pascal created a device to help his father, an accountant. He made a shoe-box-sized machine with eight wheels inside. To enter a number, the user turned a wheel. The numbers showed in windows above. Each wheel had 10 teeth. If the first wheel rotated past the tenth tooth, it would turn the second wheel one notch to the left. This carried a one over to the tens column and put a zero in

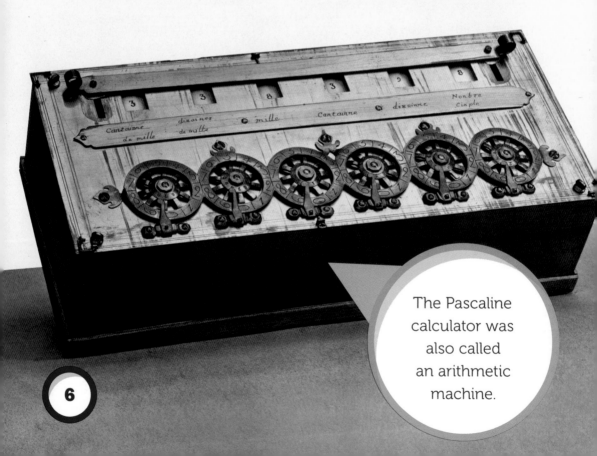

The Pascaline calculator was also called an arithmetic machine.

8

Number of wheels in the Pascaline, meaning it could calculate numbers up to eight digits long.

- Introduced by Blaise Pascal in 1642 in France.
- First automatic adding machine.
- Idea of rotating wheels still used in car odometers.

THE FIRST COMPUTERS

The word "computer" originally referred to people. Workers who spent their days making calculations were called computers. They computed data related to navigation, tide charts, and astronomy. The work was slow and repetitive. Boredom sometimes led workers to make mistakes. This led inventors to work on machines that could do the work faster and more accurately.

the ones column, just like a person would do on paper.

Pascal's invention became known as the Pascaline. The box was expensive and hard to build. It worked slowly. If the gears did not move smoothly, it could give wrong answers. But it made scientists think about how to use machines to work with numbers. It led to the creation of better, faster calculators in the years to come.

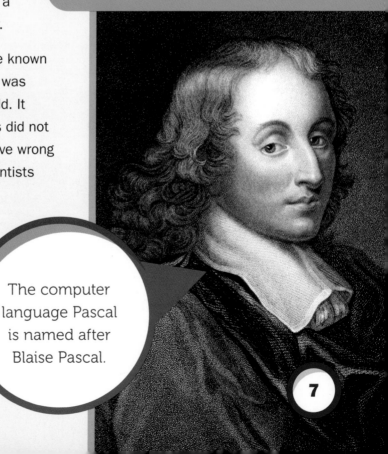

The computer language Pascal is named after Blaise Pascal.

3

JACQUARD LOOM USES PUNCHED CARDS TO RUN PROGRAMS

Before the 1800s, computers had no way to store information. That changed in 1801, when a mill owner found a way to make a loom work by itself. Joseph-Marie Jacquard punched holes in wooden cards. The holes in each card matched a line of the design. Then he strung the cards together in order. They formed a program that could be run repeatedly. The punched cards made the loom parts move up and down at the right time. The cards could be changed to make different patterns.

The Jacquard loom is used to weave textiles with complex patterns.

A machine that worked without a person was new. It meant that mills could make more cloth with fewer workers. But more than that, Jacquard's use of punched cards to store information was a breakthrough. The ability to put cards in a different order to change how they functioned is considered an early form of computer programming. Later inventors used machines with punched cards to store, process, and program information for other purposes.

11,000

Number of Jacquard looms being used in France by 1812, as the technology quickly replaced human loom operators.

- Introduced by Joseph-Marie Jacquard in 1801 in France.
- First use of punched cards to store information.
- Led to first computer programs.

THINK ABOUT IT

Some workers weren't happy when the Jacquard loom became popular. They thought they would lose their jobs if this new technology could do the work faster. Do you think more jobs are lost or gained from new technology?

TABULATING MACHINE LEADS TO MODERN COMPUTING

The US census monitors the country's population. It keeps track of ages, jobs, and other data. As the population grew, it became difficult to process so much information. In 1890, Herman Hollerith introduced

Census workers use the tabulator machine in 1940.

a machine to help. His tabulating machine used punched cards similar to those used in Jacquard's loom.

Clerks transferred data from census forms onto cards by punching holes. Then the cards were fed into a reader. Pins in the machine went through the holes and into wells of mercury below. When they touched the mercury, the pins completed electrical circuits to turn dials. Each dial tracked a different kind of data from the census.

The machine finished the job in months instead of years. It saved the government $5 million in labor in 1890. Other countries started using Hollerith's technology. Soon, it led to more complicated electronic computers. Hollerith became known as the father of modern automatic computation. His Tabulating Machine Company was renamed International Business Machines (IBM) in 1924.

80

Cards per minute a clerk could process using the tabulator.

- Introduced by Herman Hollerith in 1890 in New York.
- Used punched cards to process US census data.
- Hollerith is considered the father of modern automatic computation.

Herman Hollerith founded the computer company that became IBM.

ABC DESIGNED TO DO COMPLEX MATH

John Atanasoff taught math and physics at Iowa State University. His work involved very complicated math problems. The calculator he was using was slow and took hours to make the calculations he needed. Atanasoff teamed with a graduate student, Clifford Berry, to make a computer. They built it from 1939 to 1942. It became known as the Atanasoff-Berry Computer (ABC).

The ABC was the first all-electronic digital computer. It used binary numbers, which are combinations

The Atanasoff-Berry Computer was designed to solve complex equations.

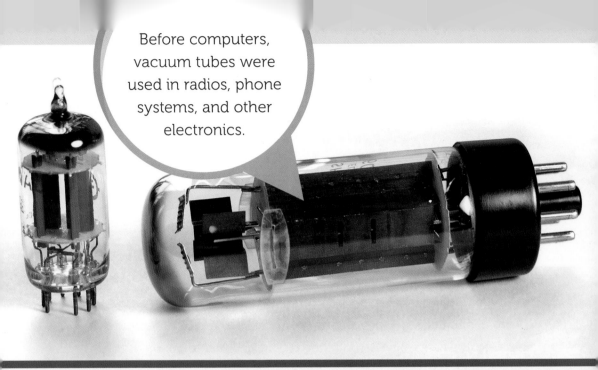

Before computers, vacuum tubes were used in radios, phone systems, and other electronics.

of ones and zeroes. The computer was as big as a desk. It weighed 700 pounds (317.5 kg). More than 300 vacuum tubes were inside. Instead of hours, it took 15 seconds to do a complicated math problem. But it could only do the math calculations for which it was designed. It couldn't store information or be programmed.

VACUUM TUBES

The first computers used small glass tubes to turn currents on or off. The air was sucked from the tube. This made a vacuum. Electricity moved through the tube. It heated a thin wire. The wire released electrons. A metal plate in the tube sent a message of "one" or "zero" depending on whether it sensed electrons.

1
Mile (1.6 km) of wire inside the ABC.

- Introduced by John Atanasoff and Clifford Berry in 1939 in Iowa.
- First to use binary numbers.
- First all-electronic computer.

HUGE ENIAC PAVES WAY FOR MODERN COMPUTERS

During World War II (1939–1945), the US Army needed a faster way to solve math problems. The government hired two experts to help. The engineers built a computer that could do 5,000 addition problems and 300 multiplication problems per second.

It was called the Electronic Numerical Integrator and Computer (ENIAC). ENIAC was fully electronic. And unlike the ABC, it was programmable. It could be adapted to different purposes.

But ENIAC had several downsides. It cost approximately $450,000 to build. It used as much power in a day as most homes used in a week. This meant it was expensive to run. It was also huge, filling a 30- by 50-foot (9- by 15-m) room. It weighed 30 tons (27 t). And it needed a lot of maintenance. Almost every day, some of the tubes burned out and had to be replaced.

ENIAC was not practical for most uses. But it gave people an idea of what computers could do. They continued trying to build smaller, better models.

18,000

Approximate number of vacuum tubes ENIAC had inside.

- Introduced by John Mauchly and J. Presper Eckert Jr. in 1946.
- Fastest computer to date.
- First computer to have memory, the capacity to store information.

A technician programs ENIAC to solve a physics problem.

7

TRANSISTORS REVOLUTIONIZE ELECTRONICS

A computer sends data through a web of switches. The first computers used vacuum tubes to do this. But the vacuum tubes were large and fragile. Scientists at Bell Labs in New Jersey hoped to find a better way. They made a small device that amplified electricity and turned it on and off. They called it a transistor.

One transistor did the work of 40 vacuum tubes. It used less power and lasted longer. It was made from solid material that was cheap and strong. It worked faster than tubes. Unlike the hot vacuum tubes, transistors stayed cool.

Transistors quickly replaced vacuum tubes in electronic devices such as radios and calculators. More people could afford to use these devices in their homes and offices. And engineers started looking for

BUGS

Grace Hopper was a programmer for the US Navy in 1947. At the time, programs were stored on long strips of paper with holes in them. Hopper found a dead moth trapped in a computer. The moth, or bug, blocked the holes in the paper and made the computer fail. Now any error that stops a computer program from working is called a bug. Fixing a computer program error is called debugging.

Before being used in computers, transistors were used in hearing aids and pocket radios.

3

Number of electrical parts in a transistor, called the source, the drain, and the gate.

- Introduced in 1947 by Bell Labs.
- Stronger, cheaper, and smaller than vacuum tubes.
- Now used in all electronic devices.

ways transistors could be used in computers. They hoped to make computers that were small and cheap enough for personal use.

TRANSISTORS FIND A HOME IN INTEGRATED CIRCUITS

Transistors made faster, cheaper, more powerful computers. But they brought new problems. To make an electrical circuit, workers had to connect each transistor by hand. Metal wires joined the transistors. Connecting lots of tiny pieces was difficult and messy. Electric currents took too long to move through wires.

In 1958, an engineer at Texas Instruments solved the problem. He made many side-by-side transistors out of one block of material. A metal layer on top joined the circuits. It was much quicker and easier to build. It was smaller and simpler, with no wires sticking out. And it worked faster.

In California, a scientist came up with the same idea. He made his integrated circuits out of silicon, an element found in sand. Another name for the invention is the silicon chip. The area of California where many computer companies started is now called Silicon Valley.

THINK ABOUT IT

Many advances in computer technology had to do with making computers smaller. Why was this important?

2000
Year Jack Kilby won a Nobel Prize for Physics for his part in inventing the integrated circuit.

- Invented by Jack Kilby and Robert Noyse in 1958.
- Connected transistors more easily.
- Led to faster, smaller computers.

Integrated circuits are also called computer chips.

INTERNET CONNECTS COMPUTERS IN WORLDWIDE NETWORK

During the 1960s, scientists and military experts wanted a secure way to share information quickly through computers. A researcher at the Massachusetts Institute of Technology (MIT) set to work on a way for computers located in different places to share data.

In 1965, another MIT scientist found a way to separate a file into blocks, called packets. The packets are sent separately, using different routes. Then the pieces are put back together when they reach the other computer. This made it possible to send information between computers without being blocked. In 1969, the scientists tried it for the first time. A computer at one college sent data to a computer at a college 350 miles (560 km) away.

The "www" at the front of web addresses stands for World Wide Web, the collection of linked pages that can be accessed through the Internet.

4

Number of computers connected by the end of 1969.

- Introduced in 1962 by MIT scientists.
- Sent data between computers for first time.
- Led to World Wide Web and e-mail.

E-MAIL

The Internet made electronic mail (e-mail) possible. E-mail lets users type messages on a computer and send them through the Internet. Messages can be sent instantly instead of waiting two to three days for a letter to be delivered. E-mail also saves paper.

At first, colleges used this technology to share research over networks. Scientists worked on connecting these networks with each other. This process was called internetting. As the number of connected networks grew, the Internet was born. By the 1980s, more people had personal computers. Companies started selling connection services and browser programs to let people access the Internet. Internet use skyrocketed during the 1990s.

The companies that connect users to the Internet are called Internet service providers.

MICROPROCESSOR LEADS TO SMALLER COMPUTERS

Integrated circuits were a big improvement over earlier computer parts. But engineers knew they could be better. Each chip did only one task. Chips had no memory. In 1971, a calculator company in Japan hired inventors at Intel to design better chips. They wanted a different chip to run each part of the calculator. The scientists at Intel had an even better idea. They put everything into one chip. It was smaller than a

As technology improves, microprocessors have gotten even tinier.

0.1

Width in inches
(3 mm) of the first
microprocessor.

- Introduced in 1971 by Intel.
- Transistors and memory contained on one chip.
- Led to much smaller, more affordable computers.

THINK ABOUT IT

Silicon chips made it possible to build smaller computers. Telephones have gotten smaller, too. What other devices have gotten smaller because of chips?

fingernail but fit 2,300 transistors. It contained everything needed to make a calculator work. Later, the same idea was used for computers.

A tiny silicon chip could do as much work as the huge ENIAC.

One of the inventors at Intel predicted that after the invention of the microprocessor, the number of transistors on integrated circuits would double every two years. So far, he has been right. Today's chips contain up to 1 billion transistors. And almost all personal computers have an Intel microprocessor inside.

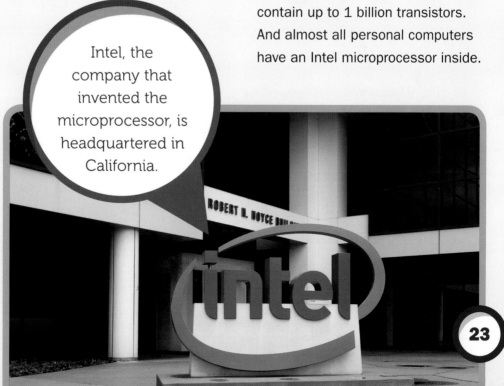

Intel, the company that invented the microprocessor, is headquartered in California.

ROBERT N. NOYCE

intel

APPLE II BRINGS PERSONAL COMPUTING TO THE MASSES

In the early 1970s, an inventor made a computer kit. It was for people who enjoyed electronics as a hobby. The kit included a microprocessor and the other parts needed to make a personal computer. The inventor hoped to sell 200. But he got orders for 2,000 kits right away. The success of the kit made

Over the years, personal computers have become sleeker and more portable.

Apple II was the first personal computer that became widely popular.

other experts see the demand for personal computers.

Two young men in California wanted to make a computer more people could use. Their idea was to make it small enough to fit on a desk. They wanted the cost to be low. They wanted it to be easy to use for those who were not scientists or engineers.

Steve Jobs and Steve Wozniak came up with the Apple II. It was a ready-made personal computer with a color display. The BASIC programming language was built in,

so it was ready to run programs. For the first time, computers were something anyone could use.

$1,298
Cost of an Apple II computer when it was introduced in 1977.

- Introduced in 1977 by Steve Wozniak and Steve Jobs.
- First user-friendly computer.
- Began the personal computer era.

SMARTPHONES LEAD TO POCKET-SIZED COMPUTING

After the widespread success of personal computers, companies started making many other electronic devices using computer technology. Personal digital assistants (PDAs) kept track of to-do lists, calendars, and phone numbers. Media players stored and played music. Photos could be viewed instantly using digital cameras. Wireless networks let computer users work and get data from the web while on the go.

At the same time, phone makers were using new technology to make handheld wireless phones. People could carry them in a purse or pocket. As computer technology such as memory and integrated circuits improved, cell phone

Many people use their smartphones to play games.

companies started making phones that were handheld computers.

IBM made the first smartphone with a touchscreen in 1993. It could be used as a calculator, address book, and calendar. Later, with better mobile phone and wireless networks, smartphones could do much more. In 2007, Apple came out with the iPhone. Soon, other companies introduced smartphones. Now a smartphone is an all-in-one device. It works as a phone and a computer. It keeps lists and calendars, takes

photos, gives directions, and plays music. Smartphone users can search for data on the Internet and video chat with friends. Now nearly 60 percent of adults in the United States own a smartphone.

Today's slender smartphones can do more than early computers that filled entire rooms.

3.95
Weight in ounces (112 g) of an iPhone 5.

- Introduced in 2007 by Apple.
- Combined many computer devices into one.
- Small and wireless.

THINK ABOUT IT

Computers have come a long way since the abacus. What do you think the next breakthrough will be?

FACT SHEET

- Computers have input and output devices. The input component lets the user enter data. A keyboard and a mouse are input devices. Earlier computers had sets of switches for inputting data. Output devices let the user get data from the computer. Monitors and printers are output devices.

- The processor is the brain of the computer. It's where data is processed. The Intel microprocessor is an example of a processor.

- Storage components let the user save data. Hard drives and CD-ROMs are storage devices. Earlier computers used floppy disks.

- Computers use software to run programs. System software is a set of step-by-step instructions that tell the computer how to work. Mac OS and Windows are types of system software. Computer programs that allow users to do different tasks are called application software. Word processors, spreadsheets, and games are types of application software.

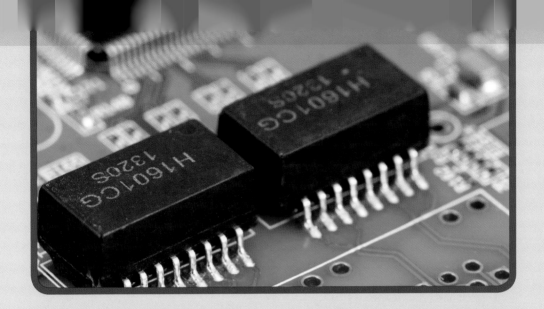

- Some computers have become so advanced that they can perform tasks associated with intelligent living things, such as learning and problem solving. This is called artificial intelligence. Deep Blue is one of the most famous examples of a computer with artificial intelligence. This IBM computer beat the world chess champion in 1997.

- Scientists and engineers continue to make breakthroughs in computer technology. Google Glass is a set of eyeglasses with a built-in computer. Users can access the Internet without their hands, using voice commands. Smart watches are like smartphones worn on the wrist.

- Wireless technology, called Wi-Fi, has let people access computers in more places than ever. Computers use radio waves to communicate with a router, which is connected to the Internet.

- Wireless technology originated in 1985, after the government made certain radio frequencies available to the public. But for years, not many people could use wireless. Devices from different manufacturers could not communicate with each other. In 1999, major companies entered into an agreement. It was called the Wireless Ethernet Compatibility Alliance. After that, wireless networks started to become more common.

GLOSSARY

amplified
Made stronger.

binary
A number system that uses combinations of ones and zeroes.

browser
A computer program used to find or look at information on the Internet.

calculator
A device used to make math calculations.

computer
A machine, usually electronic, that can store and work with large amounts of information.

data
Information in number form used by a computer.

digital
Using data in the form of numbers.

electron
A particle with a negative charge of electricity that moves around the nucleus of an atom.

electronic
Powered by the movement of electrons.

engineer
An expert who designs and builds something.

network
A system of computers or other devices that are connected to each other.

program
The instructions that tell a computer what to do.

transistor
A small device that controls the flow of electricity.

vacuum
An empty space with no air or other gas.

FOR MORE INFORMATION

Books

Computer. New York: DK Publishing, 2011.

Kops, Deborah. *Were Early Computers Really the Size of a School Bus?* Minneapolis, MN: Lerner Publications, 2011

Lemke, Donald B. *Steve Jobs, Steve Wozniak, and the Personal Computer.* North Mankato, MN: Capstone Press, 2007.

Snedden, Robert. *Who Invented the Computer?* Mankato, MN: Arcturus Publishing, 2011.

Yomtov, Nel. *Internet Inventors*. New York: Children's Press, 2013.

Websites

Computer History Museum
www.computerhistory.org

Online Safety
kids.usa.gov/teens-home/online-safety

PBS Online: A History of the Computer
www.pbs.org/nerds/timeline

INDEX

About the Author

Marne Ventura is a children's book author and a former elementary school teacher. She holds a master's degree in education with an emphasis in reading and language development from the University of California.

READ MORE FROM 12-STORY LIBRARY

Every 12-Story Library book is available in many formats, including Amazon Kindle and Apple iBooks. For more information, visit your device's store or 12StoryLibrary.com.